A souvenir guide

Townend
Cumbria

Amy Feldman

National Trust

A Lake District Village

Troutbeck village feels untouched by the modern world. Woodrow Wilson once wrote of the South Lakes, 'the very houses seem suggested by Nature and built to add to her charm'. Troutbeck exemplifies this.

The main path winding through Troutbeck village

Almost every cottage, farm and pub scattered along the meandering road through the village dates from at least the 18th century, and many are older. Their slate roofs and whitewashed walls feel as much a part of the landscape as the mountains beyond: Yoke, Ill Bell, Froswick and Thornthwaite Crag.

Then there's the surrounding farmland. Expansive, sheep-grazed fields peppered by drystone walls symbolise a landscape and community shaped by its proud agricultural heritage. Along with the characteristic Herdwick sheep, these puzzles of grey and brown stones have been a part of Cumbria's fields since the Vikings settled here in the 9th century, when they built low, circular enclosures in the valleys. Few of these remain, and the traditional walls we recognise today started taking shape after the Norman Conquest, almost a thousand years ago. The Vikings also shaped the language of the area. Streams are becks (from *bekr*), clearings 'thwaites' and hills 'fells' (*fjall*), while waterfalls are known as 'forces' (*foss*).

With so little having changed over the centuries, it's easy to imagine families of farmers living and working here 500 years ago: tending the land, breeding livestock and building up their holdings. One such family was the Brownes, farmers and residents of Townend for over 400 years and 12 generations.

With a little help from friends

Troutbeck is a close-knit community, and has been since before the Brownes' time. The family married their neighbours and also had vicious quarrels with them; they borrowed books from friends, and lent them their favourites. The neighbours also helped shape Townend: from carpets to candlesticks and portraits, many of the items that remain in Townend today were made by the Brownes' local acquaintances.

Townend

Townend may tell the story of a typical yeoman family, but its existence is anything but normal. Few historical archives and inventories of working-class families stand the test of time. Townend, however, is a treasure trove of items accumulated over the years: crockery and candleholders sit alongside 18th-century swords and intricately carved oak furniture. And then there's the Library. This collection of over 1,000 books was not simply for display: it is the everyday reading material of one family, who devoured books over dinner, splashed food on the pages and marked their places with matchsticks. As Townend's Property Manager, Emma Wright, says, it is their 'very ordinariness' that makes them 'so special and their archive such a unique survival'. Combined with receipts, letters and diaries (all of which are now held at Kendal Archive Centre), Townend provides an extraordinary insight into the lives of an ordinary family.

'I loved to wander on the Troutbeck fell. Sometimes I had with me an old sheep dog … more often I went alone. But never lonely. There was company of gentle sheep, and wild flowers and singing waters … During storms [mist] rushes down the valleys like a black curtain billowing before the wind, while the Troutbeck River thunders over the Cauldron. Memories of old unhappy far-off things and battles long ago; sorrows of yesterday and today and tomorrow the vastness of the fells covers all with a mantle of peace.'

Beatrix Potter, 'The Lonely Hills', 1942

The Brownes of Townend

The Brownes were a family of yeomen, or 'statesmen', farmers who lived at Townend from at least 1525 until 1943.

Over four centuries and 12 generations, the family continually improved their farming business, their home at Townend, and their social status; even the first known resident of Townend – and the first of eight George Brownes to own the house and farm – appears to have been well respected and influential in Troutbeck. He was chosen as one of five representatives to help define the township's boundary with Ambleside in 1552. Two years later, he was one of six 'inquisitors' who assisted the Bishop of Chester's visit to the village. George's holdings weren't the largest in Troutbeck, but were still significant: by 1558 he had the right to farm 100 cows or sheep on the village's common land (the majority of Troutbeck families were only farming five animals each at the time), and he also had a mill at nearby Limefitt.

What was a statesman farmer?

Along with many of their local contemporaries, the Brownes held their land by 'customary tenure'. Customary tenants paid an annual nominal sum to the Lord of the Manor – called 'the Lord's rent' – and had some other obligations, from defending the borders in medieval times to keeping streams and highways clear. In return, they gained freedom over what they did on their land and had the rights to much of what was on it (except woodland, game and minerals, which remained the property of the Lord of the Manor). They could also pass their property on to someone else, or it could be inherited down the family line, including widows or daughters should there be no male heir.

In the late 18th and 19th centuries, the term 'statesman farmer' began to be used to describe more successful and affluent customary tenants. They rarely referred to themselves this way though; the term was most publicised by renowned local poet, William Wordsworth. Wordsworth admired the yeomen's independence – that they were their own masters – and wrote of them in his poetry. Art critic and social thinker, John Ruskin, also respected statesman farmers, describing them as 'a scarcely injured race' that represented the true 'body and soul of England'. Though perhaps this industrious but simple, rural lifestyle appeared to be more idyllic than it really was.

Whether they thought of themselves that way or not, Troutbeck included around 50 statesman farmers. It was said to be a fiercely independent community determined to run its own affairs, even when it came to legal matters. They made a living farming sheep and cattle, and trading cloth, crops, lime, livestock, wool and, later, charcoal to fuel the iron industry at Furness. In the 17th century, the value of sheep increased and so Troutbeck, full of sheep farmers, became a relatively prosperous community. The Brownes were one of the more well-off families.

Froy Woodos
died March 1550
buried at Windermere

Christopher Browne
Ancestor of the Brownes
of Troutbeck Troutbeck

Browne
buried Nov 30th 1597

William Braun Ancestor of the Brownes of ...

Georsy
Browne
died Feb 19th 1637

Tho: Browne

George Browne
Born May 3rd 1590
died ... June 22nd 1665

Thomas Browne
died July 21st 1699
Ancestor of the Brownes of
Troutbeck, Birkrigg & Windermere

Baptd Oct 31st 1606

Ancestor of the Brownes of ...
Troutbeck

Geo. Browne
Baptd Nov 12th 1636
died Jany 16th 1703

Richard Browne
Buried Feby 10th 1669

Thomas Brenne died in London
Baptd Jany 9th 1640
Buried July 5th 1678

Madm Yor most Humble Servant
in my power Whilst Ben: Browne
Born July 22nd 1664, died Oct 5th 1748

Yor En Lo: Brethen
Richi Browne
Born March 21st 1669 lost at Sea 1708

Remains in Capt. Yr dutifull Servt
Geo: Browne
Baptd Octr 20th 1673 died in 1710 and
Buried in Flanders

Your Dutifull & Obedient
Son Ben Browne
Born Octr 2nd 1692 died ...
1748
Temple 8 Cor 25 1720

your Obedient and Dutifull Son
Rich Browne
Born Jany 24th 1697 died Augt 30th 1733
Ancestor of the Brownes of Ripon

Ever Hon.
yours
Chr Brow
27 Sept 17

died Sepr ...
Sept 12th 1767

I am Sir your most humble
Servt Geo Browne
Troutbeck 10th Jany 1766
Born Nov 2nd 1741 died Oct 11th 1806

1819
by Geo Browne
Born July 4th 1779 died ... 1830

your Dutifull Son
Benjn Browne
Born April 15th 1707 drowned in Windermere
July

Your ever kind
Jno Bro

Mrs Geo Browne
Born Jany 9th 1804 ... died June 8th 1848

George Browne

The 17th-century Brownes

The Brownes' fortune grew in the 17th century, partly due to canny business decisions and partly the result of judicious marriages.

As early as 1600, the second George Browne – son of Thomas Browne and grandson of the first George Browne – began diversifying the crops he grew. He also improved the efficiency of the family's Limefitt mill by building a weir above it, which came with its own benefits; in 1614, he caught around four hundred fish in one year. Yet these developments were not without controversy (see page 7).

A good marriage (or two)

In 1623, this George's son, a third George, married Susannah Rawlinson of Grizedale Hall in Hawkshead. Then in 1656, George and Susannah's first son – George number four – married Ellinor Fearon, the descendant of two good Cumberland families. Both unions literally changed the shape of Townend.

Susannah Rawlinson was accustomed to a higher standard of living than the Brownes' one-room farmhouse of Townend at the time. Consequently, the marriage contract required the third George to 'erect and build a new dwelling house'. We're not sure whether any improvements were made to the original farmhouse at first, but by the spring of 1650 it appears an entirely new house was being built; the Fire house is the first room to have been completed.

This was soon followed by the addition of the Downhouse – separated from the Fire house by a 'cross-passage' with a door to the front (now the Pantry) and back.

Further extensions followed George and Ellinor's marriage. By 1692, Townend had grown to include a 'bower' – or downstairs bedroom (now the Library) – a study, a buttery and six or seven loft rooms. Outbuildings included a barn, brewhouse, granary and stables.

Family fortunes

Along with the house, the family's status improved. In 1667, the fourth George – Ellinor's husband – was made High Constable of Kendal Ward (a title his son, Ben, would also hold). By 1668, George was calling himself 'gent' in 'an attempt to distinguish himself from his "less prosperous neighbours"' (Parsons, 2002). A year later, four female servants were being employed at Townend.

The Brownes also continued to grow the farm. Their flock of sheep more than doubled in size over 100 years, and by 1672 it was 229-sheep strong. In 1700, after investing in barley, the family were selling malt in near-by Ambleside, Grasmere and Patterdale. Not all their business decisions were sound: they were accused of over-coppicing, over-stocking and over-farming. Regardless, by the end of the 17th century, the family was one of the most prosperous in Troutbeck.

Right The Barn and outbuildings of Townend were built in the late 17th century as a result of George and Ellinor's marriage

The quarrelsome Brownes

The Brownes' quest for social and financial advancement meant they didn't lead the quietest of lives. In 1615, the second George Browne's weir at Limefitt mill was said to be impeding the movement of trout and salmon to and from Lake Windermere. This angered the manorial Lord – who happened to be King James I. George even had the audacity to deny the King's right to the fish in the river and fought the case, to the amazement of the lawyers.

George's descendants carried a similarly argumentative streak. In the 1650s, his grandson, the fourth George, was involved in a long and bitter dispute with William Birkett of Troutbeck Park Farm, who accused him of breaking onto his land and worrying his sheep. George claimed he was granted pasturing rights, which William denied, and the matter resulted in the two viciously attacking one another. Then in 1696, aged 70, George and two accomplices were accused of 'notoriously breaking into' a close belonging to a George Longmire – apparently with the aim of taking over his enclosure to maximise their own yield of crops.

The Brownes even quarrelled with one another. To keep his land intact, the second George decided he'd no longer split the estate between his children. In an attempt to be fair, he made his eldest son promise to share the profits from the land and rents with his brothers. After George's death, his eldest son, the third George, denied any such agreement. His brothers sued him, accusing him of 'divers cruell and wicked threats and menaces' which would impoverish them; George argued his brothers had taken advantage of memory loss he had incurred four or five years previously – a claim many considered dubious.

'Old Ben' and Elizabeth Birkett

The Brownes were already quite distinguished and prosperous when Benjamin Browne (1664–1748), or 'Old Ben', inherited Townend in 1703 – but this didn't make him any less ambitious than his predecessors.

Society was more mobile than ever before and Ben, who in 1711 followed in his father's footsteps to become high constable of Kendal Ward, aspired to the gentry. On inheriting Townend, he designed the family a coat of arms – something usually reserved for the wealthiest families – without troubling to apply to the College of Heralds. The design, featuring a double-headed eagle, can be seen on carvings in the Fire House. Some of his more extravagant household purchases included replacing Townend's old pewter, and he even sent off to Wigan near Manchester for fine spoons. He purchased three wigs and a coat once belonging to Lord Lonsdale. He added a new wing to Townend in 1739.

Ben was equally interested in bettering the family's businesses, where 'in every field he followed and improved on his father's work' (Scott, 1904). Improvements were made to the mills at Limefitt and Troutbeck Bridge, wool was spun and woven from his flock of over 200 sheep, and the value of his cattle soared. Taking advantage of the growing iron industry at Furness, Ben purchased the rights to some oak coppices and received the not-inconsiderable sum of £170 for the wood from three of them. By 1735, he had even acquired the Sun Inn pub in Lancaster, which is still there today.

Family matters

In the 18th century, the Brownes who didn't inherit Townend entered jobs that would have been considered relatively modest. Old Ben's brothers entered the army and weaving trade, and one failed to gain employment entirely. His children were more prosperous: one became an apothecary and the mayor of Kendal, another was clerk to the Board of Works at Berwick Docks, and the other became a lawyer; all careers that would have been highly regarded. In just one generation, the Brownes had noticeably moved up in the world.

Although the children's jobs may have satisfied their parents, their behaviour didn't always. George, the clerk to the Board of Works, was particularly worrisome. In 1715, Ben should have been preoccupied with defending the border from attacks by Jacobite rebels (see page 14). Yet in a letter to their son, Elizabeth writes, '[Ben] tells me with tears that all his troubles that he undergoes are not comparable to his concern hee is in about you, of your undutifullness to him, especially in your slowness in writing to him after all your misfortunes'. Despite this plea, George's correspondence never really improved.

Above 'Old Ben' was a prolific book collector, and often inscribed the title along the fore-edges of his books

Centre The Browne coat of arms designed by Benjamin Browne, featuring the double-headed eagle

Right Troutbeck church today, where Ben and Elizabeth are buried, which has been rebuilt since Ben's time

A bit of a dis-pew-t

A typical Browne, 'Old Ben' was susceptible to village disputes in his pursuit of higher status. In 1710, on learning that the reading desk in the chancel of Troutbeck church was to be removed, he sought permission from the Archbishop of York to install a new pew for his family in the vacant space, replacing his present pew in an inferior position. On 7 December, for the cost of £5, the pew was installed. However, his neighbours claimed they alone had the authority over the church's seating arrangements. And so, four days after it was installed, the villagers chopped down part of the pew, with the rest being taken out soon after.

Although Ben was later granted the right to his new seat, the villagers continued to object to the new position of items in the church. The saga continued for years, and we're still not sure whether Ben was ultimately allowed his new pew, or if he had to return to his former position.

Elizabeth Birkett

Ben's first wife, Anne, died in 1700. Two years later he re-married to Elizabeth Birkett, who lived half a mile down the road from Townend. Already over 40 years old, she probably wasn't expecting to marry or bear children. Yet in 1703 she gave birth to Christopher, who became an apothecary and mayor of Kendal.

Elizabeth is also responsible for one of Townend's most fascinating items. The 'commonplace book' is a collection of medicinal, household and culinary recipes she collated in 1699. Today it provides a fascinating insight into day-to-day life in Troutbeck: from the sort of foods enjoyed at celebrations and gatherings to common afflictions, superstitions and fears (see page 38).

The last George Browne

Over the following century, four more generations of Brownes lived at Townend. The interior of the house, however, is very much the creation and legacy of the last George Browne (1834–1914).

When George was 14, his father passed away and his mother Lucy was left to manage the farm until George was legally old enough take it on. Together they made a success of their 320 hectares (800 acres) as George was able to retire from farming aged 45, selling off some land and letting out the rest. For the last 35 years of his life, George concentrated on his personal interests: bookbinding, genealogy, gardening and, of course, the intricate oak woodcarving that fills Townend – most of which is marked with much earlier dates, as a nod to the long line of Browne descendants.

Bookbinding

George Browne was a keen amateur bookbinder and his well-worn copy of *Bookbinding for Amateurs* is kept in the Library. He was mentored by professional bookbinder and close relative William Jackson Browne, who lived with him for a number of years. Together they worked on over 100 books, mostly titles of the period, and proudly stamped their initials into each completed book. William also produced bindings on his own and it seems there were some of which he was particularly proud, as he has crossed out George's initials inside.

Carvings

George was 'a very accomplished joiner and woodcarver' (Richard Dean, former Curator of the National Trust) and no visitor to Townend could miss his carvings. They cover armchairs and bedheads, fireplaces, picture frames and mirrors. There are patterns contemporary to George and patterns that imitate more traditional, local designs. They appear to be inspired by the work of Vikings and of carvers in

Turn of phrase
Money for old rope
Historically, paper was created from white cotton or linen rags processed in a paper mill. It's said that sailors took advantage of this to make a little extra cash, selling old rope to dealers who, in turn, sold them to the paper and bookbinding trades.

Left The last George Browne, standing outside Townend's front door, in the 1870s

Right Many of George's carvings were inspired by local designs, Vikings and carvers in the South West

> 'He had a wonderful memory, and was always ready to give of his knowledge. Being possessed with a fund of dry humour, he was fond of a "crack" and would tell of happenings 60 or 70 years ago.'
>
> George Browne's obituary in the *Westmorland Gazette*, 1914

the South West. This array of styles, combined with George's tendency to carve earlier dates, makes it hard to determine exactly what work is George's, but we can make educated guesses.

Not all of George's carvings are his alone. He often worked with friends and acquaintances: 'My grandfather … went along to carve patterns on the oak there [at Townend], and I always loved to go with him, and try my hand at carving too' once remembered local resident Dorothy Bowness (*Memories of Troutbeck*).

George's legacy

The last George Browne died in 1914, succeeded by his only surviving daughter, Clara (two other daughters, Katherine and Lucy, passed away during his lifetime). On George's death, the school at Troutbeck – where he was chair of the board of governors – flew their flag at half-mast, epitomising the impact and influence of the Brownes within Troutbeck. Their legacy continues today through Townend.

Below George's tobacco jar, inscribed with his name and date, 1863

William Jackson Browne

Raised in North Yorkshire, William ran a printing and bookselling business on the edge of the North York Moors in Stokesley. When business took a turn for the worse in 1856, he spent two months in York gaol to pay off his debts.

On release, William returned home to live with his father, the vicar of Carleton-in-Cleveland. When his father died in 1866, William found himself on Townend's doorstep. Perhaps still financially wounded from the loss of his business, he offered up his bookbinding services to George and his wife, Margaret, in return for bed and board. During his time at Townend, William kept himself busy as a correspondent for the *Westmorland Gazette* and was also secretary and librarian of the Troutbeck Institute.

Margaret Browne's diary picks up his tale in January 1890, in which she chronicles William's ill health and decline over a single fortnight, until George reluctantly decided they could no longer care for his cousin. William was sent to Kendal Workhouse for medical care, where he died six days later.

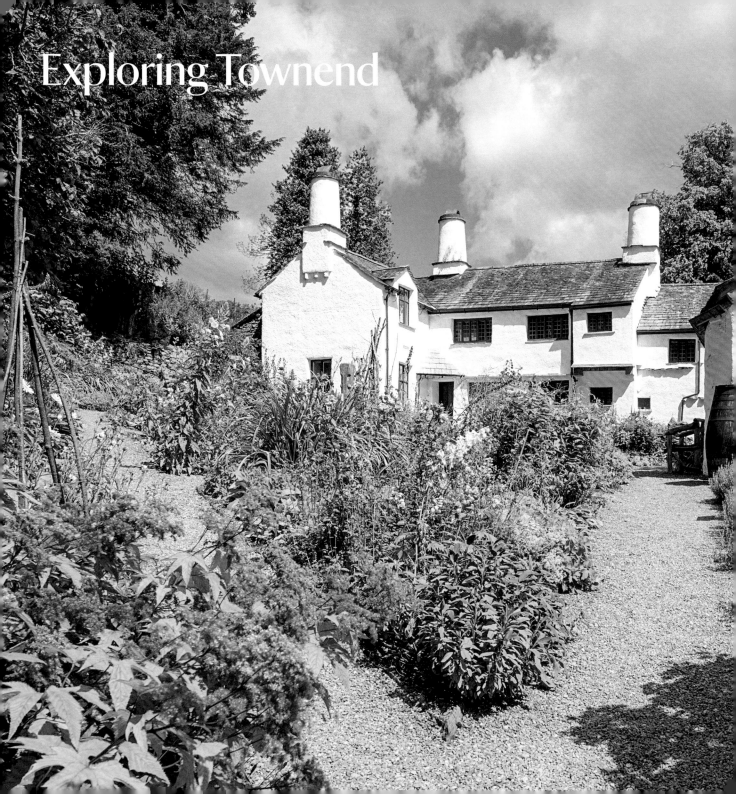

Exploring Townend

Townend today is much the same as it was in George and Clara Browne's time.

The collection of both everyday and eclectic objects is not just theirs alone, but was amassed over many centuries by the Brownes who lived here. It is, however, thanks to the father-and-daughter duo that the building, furniture and contents were lovingly preserved. They modernised little and left behind wardrobes containing Victorian dresses, cupboards packed floor-to-ceiling with cooking utensils, and baskets full of bed linen.

There's also a host of more unusual objects to be discovered, from locally painted portraits to weaponry displayed proudly on the walls, and, of course, the extensive collection of books shelved in the Library and elsewhere.

Every room and object reveals that little bit more about the lifestyle and hobbies of the many Brownes who grew up and lived at Townend, providing a glimpse into how they became one of Troutbeck's most respected and prosperous farming families.

Above The winding staircase leading up to the servants' rooms from the Mell, with the Downhouse to the right

Left Approaching Townend from the front gate with the garden in full bloom in July

The collections

The weaponry

The collection of weaponry displayed in the Fire House reflects the Lake District's turbulent political past, including when the Brownes were called to arms during the Jacobite Rebellion of 1715.

The rebellion was an attempted overthrow of the Protestant monarchy by Catholic supporters, which began in Scotland and steadily worked its way south. As the High Constable of Kendal Ward, 'Old Ben' was implored by Lord Lonsdale to 'take all possible means to preserve the Country from rapine and plunder'. Ben procured arms and spent almost the entirety of October 1715 raising an army. 'Hee is scarce a day at Home in a fortnight,' despaired his wife, Elizabeth. After some tense near misses at Kendal and Kirkby Lonsdale, the invasion was unsuccessful; Ben and his troops were granted a safe return to Troutbeck.

Townend has four swords in its collection, along with a wooden pike dating from the late 16th to early 17th century, bullet moulds and handcuffs that were used by 'Old Ben' in his role as High Constable.

Longmire's landscapes

There are more paintings of sheep at Townend than there are of family and friends; such was the animal's importance to the Brownes, especially the last George. They are by George's friend and local farmer-cum-artist, William Taylor Longmire (1841–1914).

Longmire is thought responsible for the small portrait of George as an adult in the State Bedroom, though he is better known as a landscape painter and produced a number of views of the Lake District. He had quite an unusual method. Working on around 20 pictures at once, he painted one colour on each canvas, then added the next, building them up colour by colour. A number of his landscapes can be seen around Townend including a watercolour of the exterior of Townend, in which a peacock struts in the garden. There are also some of Longmire's oil paintings. One shows two sheep facing one another with Troutbeck church in the distance. Another – in what feels like a departure from his usual style – depicts wild boar hunting.

The candleholder

Electric lighting was never installed at Townend during the Brownes' time; even Clara, who was here until her death in 1943, chose to use paraffin oil lamps. So dotted around Townend are portable lights, once used to carry out intricate tasks after sundown.

The Downhouse holds the 'star of the lighting collection' (Dillon, 2014). This rare, wrought-iron piece was primarily a candleholder, but rarely used as such. Candles were hugely expensive in the 18th century and reserved for entertaining only the most distinguished of guests. On a typical day, Ben and his family would have burned rushlights, held by the two v-shaped holders. Far more affordable than candles, these were made by soaking the dried pith of a rush plant in animal fat or grease; when lit they burned for just under an hour.

Turn of phrase

Burning the candle at both ends

When held at an angle, rushlights could be lit at both ends. This gave twice the light but also meant they burnt out twice as quickly. Nowadays the phrase means to live your life in the fast lane, to work (or play) hard at both ends of the day – something that could quickly lead to feeling 'burnt out'.

Chapbooks

Particularly popular from the 17th to 19th century, chapbooks were small, inexpensive, populist titles sold by travelling traders called 'chapmen'. They were so cheaply produced that few chapbooks survive today, making Townend's collection all the more remarkable.

Chapbooks were enduringly popular with the Brownes: Townend holds bound collections belonging to three generations of Georges (b.1779, 1804 and 1834), and some that once belonged to Lucy Walker.

Stories range from the bawdy to the tragic. In *The Crafty Chambermaid's Garland* (Newcastle, 1770), a rich merchant attempts to seduce his mother's maid. Knowing he isn't interested in marriage, the maid tricks the merchant by inviting him to bed, but hides a 'bunter' (very ugly woman) in her place, scaring off the merchant. Her trick amuses the merchant's family so much that they allow her to marry him despite their contrasting backgrounds. More harrowing is *The Devonshire Garland,* the story of young daughter sent away after being impregnated by her father and the subsequent tragedies that befall her – including her unwitting marriage to her own son.

Lucy Browne's wedding dress

Lucy Browne, neé Walker (d.1862) was the mother of the last George Browne. In June 1832, she and George's father, another George, were married in Bowness. For the occasion, Lucy wore this honey-coloured silk brocade day dress and matching cape, both embroidered with tiny flowers.

The size of the dress indicates just how short and petite Lucy was; the waist measures just 17 inches. This beautiful dress is now nearing the end of its life and, despite our best conservation efforts, it is likely that damage from light, gravity and dust will eventually mean that the fabric falls apart and we will no longer be able to display it.

The Downhouse

The Downhouse was the working heart of Townend. Huge, thick, slate floor flags are worn around the edges from centuries of being trodden by the busy Brownes and their servants.

Hanging from the ceiling are iron pots and pans used for rustling up meals, clap bread and rubbery 'wang cheese', which would then be carefully suspended above the flames with adjustable hooks (known as 'ratten crooks') in the fireplace. It was in front of this fire that Clara Browne spent her latter years, relaxing in her armchair.

As with many of the rooms at Townend, it's George Browne's presence that is most strongly felt here – and not just in the wooden carvings. A map of Westmorland hangs on the wall, the new 1847 railway line added by hand. Plaques celebrating his prize-winning sheep are displayed proudly. A personalised cherub-emblazoned tobacco jar sits above the fireplace.

This room was built in the mid- to late 17th century, following the completion of neighbouring Fire House. It is known as the 'Downhouse' because of its position a few steps down from the other room. In poorer houses, animals would be brought into the Downhouse during winter and the steps helped to contain the muck in this space.

Clap bread
Although wheat wouldn't grow successfully in this area, oats were plentiful and so a common food was 'clap bread'. This was essentially a thin, hard oat cake which could be up to one foot in diameter, cooked on a griddle and then dried out on a rack. If well made, it was 'as crisp and pleasant to eat as anything you can imagine' (*A Tour of the Westmorland Lakes*, 1697). It was supposedly given its name as it was 'clapped' into shape before baking.

The meat loft

Situated directly above the fireplace and accessed from one of the maid's bedrooms on the first floor, this is where meat was hung to dry and be preserved. Large cuts of mutton and 'buttacks of beef' were strung on the hooks, and smoke, which preserved the meat, was channelled upwards from the fire below (smoked mutton was known as 'macon').

The cuts would be particularly plentiful in autumn, when the family stocked up in preparation for the winter, when their animals weren't farmed – there might have been as much as £700-worth of meat (in today's money) hanging there at any one time.

The 'fitted kitchen'

This characterful array of boxes, shelves, cupboards and even a Bible Box was fitted together by the last George Browne towards the end of the 19th century (though many of the individual pieces pre-date this). It is perhaps one of the earliest examples of a 'fitted kitchen'. George was also responsible for the shelves, beading and carved details on many of the panels.

Dating from 1740, the eight-day longcase calendar clock is one of the more unusual additions and was supposedly gifted to the second Ben Browne by its maker, William Wilson of Kendal, in exchange for some legal advice.

Katie's chair

Sitting by the fireside, this miniature oak elbow chair was carved by George Browne for his youngest daughter, Katie, for her fourth birthday; her initials 'KMB' and the year, 1873, feature at the top.

The weaver's bowl

This rare survival dating from around 1800 is a curious object to us now, but glass light intensifiers were not uncommon in 19th-century homes. They were used for carrying out intricate

tasks such as reading, sewing or weaving after dark. The bowl was filled with water and a lit candle was placed behind; the bowl then diffused the light.

The plaques

Around the door hang the plaques won by George Browne's Herdwick sheep in the Royal Agricultural Society of England's 1879 International Exhibition (the show catalogue is in the Library). The sheep had to be transported to London on the train from Windermere, but it was worth the effort. George came second with 'Patch' in class 182 ('a ram of any other age') and an unknown sheep in class 181 ('shearling ram'), winning a £5 prize for each. He went one better in class 183, 'a pen of five shearling yews', taking home first place and a £10 prize.

The Mell

As you go up the steps out of the Downhouse, you find yourself in a small area known as the 'mell'. Here you can see the old 'cross-passage' between the Downhouse and Fire House, with a door to the front (now the pantry) and back.

Above The weaver's bowl; a rare survival dating from around 1800

Left Detail of the elaborate carvings in the 'fitted kitchen' in the Downhouse, created by the last George Browne

The Fire House

This heavily panelled, 17th-century room is the oldest part of Townend. For centuries, family and servants, farm hands and boarders gathered around the board table to eat and drink, entertain and be entertained.

'Fire House' is the traditional local name for the main heated room on the ground floor. For generations the eponymous fire burned constantly, providing light as well as warmth.

The fireplace and surrounds

Although it has been adapted and modernised over the years, the fireplace was installed when this room was first built in 1650. Originally it would have been an open hearth and set further back in the room; a place to sit and keep warm while cooking (it was common to wear a hat when doing this, to prevent soot, or 'hallan drop', landing on your head). The hearth was modernised by the seventh George Browne in

Above The fireplace was an original feature of Fire House, first built in 1650, and then later modernised in the 19th century by the seventh George Browne

1842–43, installing the Gothic chimney piece, cast-iron grate and panelling. Although the panel work itself is from the 1670s, we think it was brought here at a later date.

Some older features remain. The spice cupboard to the right and press cupboard to the left of the fireplace were installed in 1672. The top half of the press cupboard was used to store pewter and lock away silver. 'Clapbread' (see page 16) was kept in the bottom; one batch could feed a family for a month.

The table

The 17th-century board table and its benches were assembled in this room some time before 1731. Its vast size – to accommodate entire families, their servants and guests – has been grabbing attention ever since. Underneath are wooden stretchers, where feet could be rested away from the chilly flagstones. At one end, the stretcher is almost entirely worn away. The reason as to why is something of a mystery; perhaps it was deliberately lowered to accommodate longer legs, or maybe it was worn away over centuries of use.

Turn of phrase
Board tables

The earliest western dining tables were 'board tables' – wooden boards placed on trestles. These have borne a number of phrases, from 'board games' (games played at a table) to 'bed and board' (breakfast or dinner might be served to guests at the large board table), 'treading the boards' when used as an impromptu stage, and even 'chairman of the board', as the head of the table would sit on the only chair round the table while everyone else sat on benches.

Christopher's pill slab

Christopher Browne (1703–47) was the only child of Elizabeth Birkett and 'Old Ben' (Ben's other children were born to his first wife, Ann). He moved to Kendal and became an apothecary; then in 1734 the town's mayor.

This blue-and-white ceramic pill slab belonged to Christopher, but he probably didn't use it to make medicines. Instead many such slabs were hung as window displays. It features the arms of the Worshipful Society of Apothecaries and their motto in Latin, taken from Ovid's *Metamorphoses*, which roughly translates as 'I am spoken of all over the world as one who brings help'.

Christopher's generation of apothecaries was perhaps the last to display slabs like this. From about 1750 they lost popularity, replaced by white tiles more likely used for pill making than décor.

George's carvings

The work of the last George Browne features heavily in this room, although the dates engraved would have you believe otherwise. Inscribed at the top of the bookcase is 'GBE 1687' (George and Ellinor Browne), but we have drawing plans dated from 3 December 1887, so we know the earlier carved date is false. Similarly, an armchair is marked 'BBE1702' (Old Ben and Elizabeth Browne), but we know it was George who embellished each chair with the coats of arms. Two branches of the Brownes feature: eagles for the English and lions' paws for the family from Ireland and Essex. But there are also other prominent Westmorland families, suggesting George was trying to ally himself with them: the Braithwaites of Ambleside's hunting horn and the Birketts' wheat sheaves.

This collection of 1,331 ordinary books belonging to an ordinary yeoman family is the only surviving library of its kind in the world.

In 1975, historian J. D. Marshall claimed that 'the probate inventories of the regional yeoman was typically and notoriously lacking in many books beyond the Holy Bible'. Townend turns that common misconception upside down. The books in the Library – 44 of which are totally unique to Townend – include titles on law and politics, in Greek and in Latin. These sit alongside childhood tales and bawdy chapbooks – as well as seven different editions of the Bible. The earliest book is a 1548 copy of Erasmus's *Paraphrases in Novum Testamentum* in Latin; the final addition was Clara Browne's copy of *Pied Piper* (London, 1942).

The well-thumbed books were not just intended for display: corners are turned over, pages are annotated and splashed with mud; in one, a place is marked with a matchstick. The books were also lent to and borrowed from neighbours. One book, which the family borrowed from Troutbeck Institute in 1888, has never been returned. 'Old Ben' was more meticulous about remembering the titles he gave out, noting them in his diary. So the Townend library also shows that the Brownes weren't unusual among local people in being keen readers. In fact, nearby Kendal even had a flourishing book trade and there was a lending library there by the 1750s.

No wonder Mark Purcell, former Libraries Curator for the National Trust, said that Townend's Library 'changes your view of what 17th-century England was like'.

Building the Library

This room hasn't always been a dedicated library. It was first built after the fourth George married Ellinor Fearon around 1672 and used as a downstairs bedroom. Back then, books would have been stored in chests. Unlike in most homes and libraries today, the pages, rather than the spine, faced outwards; it's still possible to see where former owners have inked on the title for easy identification.

The display of books as seen today was, like much of Townend, the work of the last George Browne.

'Old Ben' the collector

Townend's most prolific book collectors were the two Ben Brownes. 'Old Ben' was arguably pioneering in the way he acquired his 142 books. Formal book auctions had only been held in London since 1676, but just 31 years later Ben was attending them in Cumbria. 'Young Ben' also sent him a number of books from London, where he was working. The titles are predominantly about religion and the law and were perhaps used in 'Old Ben's' work as High Constable.

Another unusual aspect of Ben's collection is the way in which he inscribes his signature, often alongside the date and price of purchase, into bookbindings.

The books

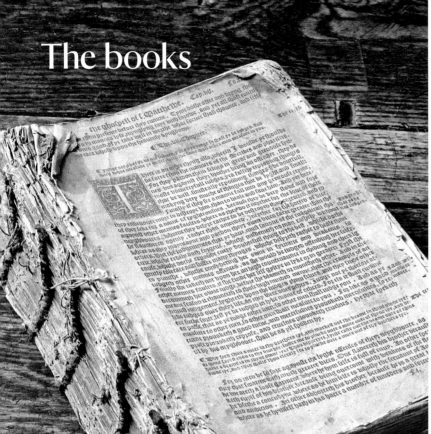

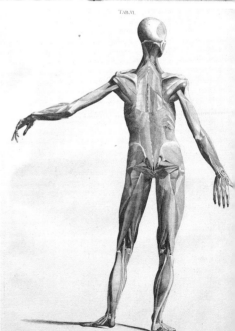

The books at Townend help tell the Brownes' story: a tale of an ordinary family with many and varied interests and values, keen to move up the social order.

They used literature to 'better' themselves, both intellectually and socially. They read histories about the local area and about Europe. They collected poetry and Shakespeare, political plays and comedies. They procured recipe and hymn tomes, and used books to get them through the toughest of times: a copy of *A Token for Mourners* was purchased in 1700, the year 'Old Ben' and Anne's baby daughter died.

Keeping up with the Joneses

The Brownes actively pursued a higher social status and this is reflected in their book collection. In the mid-17th century, George, husband of Ellinor, was reading *A Way to Get Wealth* (London, 1648), which advises on gentlemanly activities, preparing banquets and feasts, making orchards and 'husbanding' bees. George's copy is a seventh edition, suggesting he was not alone in his desire to better himself. Somewhat ironically, George also owned a copy of *The Art of Contentment* (1675), which advises that contentment can be found by 'mortifying our pride' and asking yourself whether you would give up all you have now for that which you desire. The Library also houses 19th-century copies of *Burke's Peerage and Baronetage* (1857) and *London Society*.

The political and the gory

The Brownes were clearly keen to keep up with current affairs. There are books about Europe, including one on 'the various interests of princes, their several claims, disputes and intrigues' (1716). Another recounts the trials of 29 men accused of the 'regicide of Charles I', published the same year as the trials (1660) – more current affairs than history. The son of 'Young Ben', George Browne

(b.1741) was also interested in 'true crime'. His copy of *The Tyburn Chronicles* (London, 1768) details misdemeanours having taken place from 1700 to the then present day, including bigamy, piracy, highway robberies, murders and treason. One story features the lucky escape of John Smith who was tried at the Old Bailey in 1705 for stealing 148 pairs of gloves and 22 stockings from a shop. He was sentenced to death and hanged for 15 minutes, until a bystander's new evidence granted him a reprieve and he was cut down.

Benjamin Browne and his medical texts

Many of the medical books in the Library were the leading texts of their day. They belonged to the grandson of 'Young Ben', another Benjamin (b.1787).

Benjamin studied to become a surgeon and apothecary following his father's death in 1804; left £200, Benjamin arranged to be apprenticed to Dr William Simpson of Ambleside. Before he'd fully served his apprenticeship, Dr Simpson passed away suddenly, aged just 34, and Benjamin was released. He went to study in Edinburgh, completed his education and returned to take over Dr Simpson's practice in Ambleside in 1807. Tragically, that same year he died in a sailing accident on Windermere.

But Benjamin's story doesn't end there. On the 22 March 1808, a baptism is recorded of 'George, son of Agnes Simpson, Widow of the late William Simpson Surgeon, born on the 18th, a Bastard, the late Benjamin Browne, Surgeon, the reputed Father'. It seems Benjamin took over from his old master in more ways than one.

Remnants of Rhyme

Another well-known Troutbeck resident was Thomas Hoggart, or 'Auld Hoggart', uncle to the satirist William Hogarth. Hoggart was a poet and playwright and has a similarly satirical style to his nephew. A copy of his *Remnants of Rhyme* can be found in the Library.

The Landing
The State Bedroom

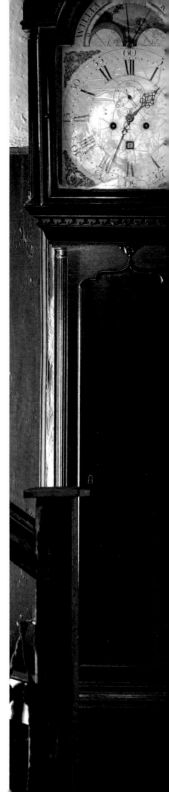

The Landing

On reaching the first floor, it might appear that you can continue on to explore more rooms above using the next staircase. You can't. Not because this is an area closed to the public, but because there are no such rooms: the staircase simply leads to a small space under the roof.

We're not sure who installed this mysterious staircase. It dates to the 17th century but could have been purchased and installed here much later by the last George. Regardless, it highlights the Brownes' endless concern with appearance: as such a staircase would have been impractical, it was probably installed simply to make the house appear grander than it really is.

The State Bedroom

This space provided guest accommodation for the Brownes' most important guests and also occasionally for family members.

The wood carvings

Unsurprisingly the last George Browne, who surveys the room from the (arguably quite crude) 1868 oil painting by the window, is responsible for much of the wood craftsmanship in this room. Rosettes and leaves adorn the washstand; muscular figures prop up the coats of arms flanking the fireplace; intricate, intertwined oak leaves surround the mirror (one of George's rare honestly dated pieces, from 1881).

The state bed

Although the showpiece bed pre-dates George, he did add his signature touch to some of the nine headboard panels and its footboard. Beatrix Potter, who owned a nearby farm and was known to visit Clara at Townend, despaired of his additions: 'Alas! Old Miss Browne's father was an enthusiastic carver in the bad Victorian days when amateurs "improved" old oak,' she

Left Inside the State Bedroom

Right View through to the State Bedroom from the Landing. The grandfather clock is by William Wilson of Kendal, and would have originally displayed the tides and phases of the moon

wrote in 1940. 'Foot boards of the splendid old bedstead have been covered with copied patterns by the tiresome Mr Browne.'

Beatrix wasn't necessarily as adept in spotting George's work as she might have thought; the snake detailing on a headboard panel – which she said could have been 'the worm Midgard' or 'an ordinary local adder' which she believed to be original is probably actually George's work.

The bed hangings aren't original, but using details from old photographs, have been specially woven to recreate what once hung here.

The cradle

Dated to 'GBE' (George and Ellinor Browne) and 1670, the oak cradle at the foot of the bed is probably one of the few accurately dated older pieces in the house. It's likely every Browne baby from that date onwards slept here. From the turned spindles that spiral upwards to support the cradle's wooden tester, to the interlacing designs sweeping along the side panels, the cradle isn't short of striking designs.

The Picture Room

The Picture Room opposite the stairs would have been a bedroom for extended family, and is currently used as an exhibition space. It contains family photographs of the last George Browne and his three daughters.

Turn of phrase
Daylight robbery
When the 'window tax' was introduced, many homeowners bricked up all but six windows to avoid paying the levy. One theory is that, as this prevented sunlight getting to some rooms, the tax was referred to as 'daylight robbery'.

The Blue Bedroom
The Main Bedroom

The Blue Bedroom

This sky-blue room may have had a couple of purposes. Next to the door is a fitted linen cupboard, installed by George and Ellinor in 1672 to fill an opening that may have housed an earlier staircase coming up from the Fire House. Alongside this cupboard is the linen closet, now used to display Lucy Browne's wedding dress from 1832 (see page 15).

At the opposite end of the bedroom, next to the large front window, is the space Ben Browne described as 'ye Clossett over my Entery into ye House' in 1732. Containing a desk, this was formerly used as an office.

The large, un-level oak floorboards in this room are original. Note the pegs nailing them in to shape: quite literally square pegs in round holes.

The Main Bedroom

Described as 'my Room Over the House' by Old Ben in 1731, this was the domain of Townend's master and mistress. Its position at the front of the house – overlooking the courtyard and garden – made it the perfect place from which to survey the comings and goings of Townend and Troutbeck.

It's also said that Clara Browne sometimes hosted bed and breakfast guests here, leaving them water glasses and a carafe in the little cupboard.

Right Inside the Main Bedroom; the furniture and fittings are decorated with George Browne's carvings

Recreating the past

The detailed, screen-printed wallpaper in this room isn't original, but is a replica of what was here in Victorian times. It was recreated using a small fragment found lining the cupboard, and black-and-white photographs that show how the room used to look. Both here and in the State Bedroom, the bed hangings are specially produced copies based on old photographs.

The carvings

Like most rooms at Townend, the last George Browne's carvings feature heavily in this room; from the decorative details on the 17th-century bed to the vines trailing around the mirror (the latter is one of eight in the house to which George has added his mark). The fact that the Brownes owned so many mirrors also highlights the family's prosperity. In the 18th century especially, looking glasses were not an everyday household item and only afforded by the wealthy – or those who wanted to appear so.

The fire surround is also perhaps one of the most 'honest' items in the property. Not only does it feature a true date and the initials of the last George Browne and his wife, Margaret, but also the patterns are typical of George's era, rather than aping designs from earlier works. Look out for the long row of carved faces that run the full length of the fireplace.

The superstitious Brownes

In 2009, a horseshoe was found underneath the floorboards adjacent to the window. The Brownes would have placed this here to protect the household from evil spirits, who they believed could enter through doors, windows and chimneys. Never removed, it still protects the house today.

One of the room's most striking features is how the floor slopes steeply up from the door. Specially made furniture accommodates this: the bed and dressing table's legs are slightly longer on one side than the other to ensure they, at least, lie flat.

Presiding over the room is a three-quarter-length oil painting of the last George Browne aged eight. In it he clutches a riding crop, and this can still be seen by the window in the Fire House. Although we don't know who the artist was, it's clearly an expensive, high-quality painting, showing how valued George was to his parents; as an only child, the responsibility for continuing the long line of Brownes rested with him.

Above Portrait of George Browne as a young boy, c.1842

The servants' bedrooms

The servants' bedrooms

Accessed from the Downhouse, these three more modestly furnished rooms were where the maids and housekeeper slept: the former in the two smaller rooms, and the latter in the larger. At various times they also probably housed guests and the Brownes' children, particularly from the mid-18th century when it became less common for a family to share one big room. At this point, the servants may have all moved in to the attic space above.

The right-hand maid's bedroom also provides access into the Downhouse meat loft.

The housekeeper's bed

Beds such as the one in the housekeeper's room are known as rope beds. Instead of having wooden slats to hold a mattress as you would today, beds were supported by ropes, which are visible in the footboard. These had to be tightened frequently to keep the mattress comfortable. A common belief is that this is how the phrase 'sleep tight' originated. In reality, the phrase isn't recorded as having been used until long after ropes had been replaced by metal straps and springs, so this probably isn't the case.

'Recycled' furniture

The wardrobes in the housekeeper's bedroom were originally chests known as kists used for storing oats and barley. When this room was turned into a servants' room, their purpose changed too: they were turned on to their ends and pegs were fitted inside for hanging clothes.

The Felon's Loft

In the late 17th and early 18th centuries, this space – situated above the servants' bedroom and accessible via a ladder – was used by High Constables 'Old Ben' and George to hold criminals before they were tried. We think the area was split in two, with an inner half to keep the felons and an outer half where the male servants – or 'hinds' – slept, perhaps to protect the female servants below from any potential escapees. Chests used for storing oats and barley would also have been found here.

Right Inside one of the servants' bedrooms above the Downhouse

Left The housekeeper's bed, as seen through the doorway of the, much smaller, maid's room

The garden

Townend's informal, cosy cottage-style garden is very similar to the one the last George Browne enjoyed in the early 20th century, right down to the sweeping, awe-inspiring views of Troutbeck valley.

Here there are elements to catch the eye throughout the year, from splashes of snowdrops in early spring to the dahlias and hydrangeas that linger until autumn. However, it's in late spring and summer, when riotous colour sweeps through the borders and courtyard, that Townend's garden is at its glorious best.

These bright plants reflect the garden designed by the last George. As passionate about his garden as his house, George's records of what he planted here are meticulous. He noted what worked and what didn't, and produced lists of 'troublesome weeds' such as 'Willarherb' (rosebay willowherb) and planting schemes. Favourite plants appear to have been his prize-winning pansies and sweet peas, the latter of which he grew 19 varieties. He also grew 28 different types of phlox, all planted in alphabetical order. George's love of plants must have been well known in Troutbeck as he writes about how people brought him plants and flowers to try out in the garden.

Below The front gate surrounded by colourful border planting in July

The meadow and orchard

By the car park is a wildflower meadow filled with narcissi, dog's tooth violets, snakes head fritillaries and, a more recent introduction, yellow rattle.

Above the path is the highest part of the garden that sits atop a long, steeply sloping bank. Here yew trees planted in 1736 shelter an orchard planted by the last George. Although this no longer houses the 20 varieties of fruit to which George tended, the apples, damsons, pears and plums still abound in autumn.

The lower garden

Once home to livestock, horses and another small building (replaced with planting during the last George's time), the courtyard is a more peaceful spot today. In spring, the air is perfumed by coconut-scented gorse, which gives way to hollyhocks, day lilies and lady's mantle in June. The latter was once a popular medicinal herb; the roots and leaves were used for bruises and to heal wounds, while tea made from it was said to relieve menstrual pain.

In summer, the herbaceous borders burst with vibrant red oriental poppies and aptly named sweet-rocket, so-called for its enticing aroma. Among the other plants here is comfrey, a handy herb that can be steeped in water to make a fertiliser. It was also traditionally used to treat a huge range of ailments including acne, arthritis, broken bones, sprains, and severe burns.

Dahlias provide a boost of colour to the cut-flower border from July to October, and in summer they're joined by delicate sweet peas and their intoxicating perfume. Roses appear from May to October. These also attract deer, who enjoying snacking on them (despite our best efforts to keep them out!).

The sundial

Dating from 1766, the sundial plinth sitting in the centre of the garden was made for the fifth George Browne, born in 1741. It was moved to its current position by the last George when he developed the plan on which the current garden's design is based.

Above left Bright pink lupins stand out against the white-washed walls of the house

Above right Roses appear in the garden from May to October

What's different today?

Although the garden is as similar as possible to its Victorian design, we have had to make some adaptations. Black spot and other diseases affect many of the historic breeds of roses that George grew, making them too difficult to grow today. Others simply will no longer flourish in the poor, stony soil.

We've also introduced a few plants that George wouldn't have recognised to help attract more wildlife to the garden, such as verbena. The valerian next to the information room is a favourite with many species, particularly the hummingbird hawk-moth.

Farming and the Valley

Hill farming is integral to the Lake District. The agricultural tradition has shaped communities, the economy and landscape.

Drystone walls are as much a part of the outlook as the area's craggy mountains, green hills and eponymous rich-blue lakes. In return, the challenging land has shaped Lake District farming. Ninety per cent of Cumbria's 'Less Favoured Areas' of land are here; consequently farmers favour livestock over crops and the locally treasured Herdwick sheep is known for its hardiness.

Townend has long been part of this tradition. The Brownes farmed sheep and cattle on around 320 hectares (800 acres), from low-level land in Troutbeck village to higher ground at Wansfell and the top of the Kirkstone Pass.

Farming at Townend today

Today the Brownes' farmland is owned by the National Trust and managed by tenant farmers. The Freemans, who have been here for over forty years, now look after a larger area than the Brownes did, combining National Trust land with their own. Like the Brownes, they produce Swaledale sheep but also Luing and pedigree Limousin cattle, and cross-bred, blue-faced Leicester sheep (lowland rams are crossed with upland ewes to produce sheep hardy enough to survive on the fells, but able to raise more than one lamb). Each year, over 600 lambs are born on their land.

The Barn (not open to the public)

Sitting over the road from the farmhouse and visible from the garden is Townend's slate-and-stone bank barn. First built in 1666, it's one of the few working barns remaining in Troutbeck today. Here cattle were stalled, wood and oats dried and even a small carriage stored. Wool was kept in a partitioned-off 'room' and farmhands slept in the wings at either end. Housed downstairs, dogs provided a deterrent to rustlers. The barn could also be used for crop farming: opening the doors at each side created a draught, which separated the corn from the chaff. Over 350 years later, the barn continues to be used for agriculture, including lambing. It also houses sheep and, just like in the Brownes' days, hay is stored in the loft.

As with their farmhouse, the Brownes extended the original 1666 barn to make it into a well-equipped building befitting a well-off statesman farmer. Over the years the doors have been enlarged to accommodate first horse-drawn vehicles and tools, and latterly larger machinery, and improvements have been made to all but one cattle stall.

Left Swaledale sheep grazing on the fells of the tenanted farmland once belonging to the Brownes

The spinning gallery

The spinning gallery is a typical feature of Lake District barns, but also something of a misnomer. Instead of spinning, most were used for drying fleece, flax and other products which may have been displayed for the benefit of the travelling tradesmen, who traversed the countryside with their servants seeking spun yarn and woven cloth. The gallery also provided a way through from one end of the upper floor to the other when the barn was full.

The Brownes' farming year

Up until the 1940s, hill farmers' lives were dominated by the seasons. Even now, while processes and technology may have changed, some month-by-month activities remain the same. November is a time for new beginnings: it marks the traditional start of the Celtic year, but also mating season for sheep. Rams become so excitable that they might jump five-foot-high walls and challenge each other head-on. Lambs are born in April, their arrival carefully planned to ensure they aren't exposed to the harsh winter climate of earlier months.

Some things have changed: today, sheep are treated for lice and parasites in February but in the past this would have taken place in autumn, the animals treated with a mixture of butter and tar rubbed into their skin. In Cumbria, traditionally the harvest of hay and cereals took place in August and was undertaken using a sickle. In his 1800 guidebook to the Lake District, John Housman claimed that a Cumbrian girl could reap more corn in a day than any labouring man in the southern counties.

Left The barn was first built in 1666, and is one of the few working barns in Troutbeck today

The Final Browne Years

Townend remained the Browne family home until Clara Browne's death in 1943.

The only surviving daughter of the last George Browne, Clara lived alone at Townend, occasionally taking bed and breakfast guests who stayed in the Main Bedroom.

Having never married and with no children of her own, Clara's closest relations were Richard and William Browne – first cousins on her mother's side, and second cousins on her father's. The brothers lived at Townend for some years after the death of their parents in the mid-1880s. William trained as a butcher in Ambleside before emigrating to New Zealand, where he established a successful business in Thames, not far from Auckland. It was to him that Clara left the Townend estate.

'All this should never have happened, for there are now no more Brownes of Townend.'

Gilbert Browne, 1944

Cataloguing Townend
One of Hedley's stipulations was that all Townend's contents were properly catalogued. Along with his daughter, Philippa, Canon Luard-Selby began to visit each afternoon to undertake the long process, discovering everything from dresses in a closet to family letters, which, as a classical scholar, he could transcribe. This revealed stories such as Ben riding through two pairs of breeches and re-shoeing his horse twice on the journey from Kendal to London.

After Clara

In 1944, a year after Clara's death, Richard and his wife, Leonora, arrived from New Zealand to begin life in their new house. Although Richard had grown up in Troutbeck, it appears he may have mis-remembered Townend. Initial enchantment was swiftly followed by disillusionment as they realised that the rambling, un-modernised house – with no electricity or piped water – was no place in which to enjoy their retirement. Failing health and harsh winters prompted the couple to sell the property and return to New Zealand, though sadly Richard never made it back. He died on board ship and was buried at sea.

Another second cousin, Gilbert, was a colonial civil servant who used to visit Clara when at home on leave. When the property was put on the market by Richard, Gilbert was incommunicado in South Africa. His wife, Sadie, knew of his love of Townend and sought to buy it. But it was not to be. On visiting her solicitor to finalise arrangements, he informed Sadie that he had just visited Townend and found a notice pinned on the door saying the property had been sold the previous night. The family were devastated: 'all this should never have happened, for there are now no more Brownes of Townend', lamented Gilbert in November 1944.

Oswald Hedley

Townend's new owner was coal magnate Oswald Hedley, who paid £5000 for the house and an equal sum for the majority of the farmland. Oswald already owned several properties in the Windermere Valley and nearby Fell Foot (now also National Trust). He didn't plan to use Townend himself, but instead intended it as a retirement home for his close friend and Troutbeck vicar, Canon Luard-Selby.

Then in his sixties, Canon Luard-Selby had crippling arthritis and glaucoma. He lived in the large vicarage, and with no house of his own or a

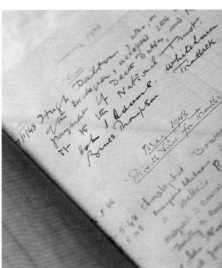

pension, he couldn't leave his role. The gift of Townend must have been a huge relief.

But Canon Luard-Selby never moved in. Oswald Hedley died suddenly on Christmas Eve 1945, aged 61. His wife, Edith, had to transfer ownership of the estate to the Treasury in part-payment of death duties. The sum raised by the house and farmland only met about 1/30th of the sum required. Canon Luard-Selby continued as vicar of Troutbeck until his death in 1951.

The National Trust comes to Townend

On receiving the Townend estate from Edith Hedley, the Treasury then made it over to the National Trust. The contents were purchased separately, from the Hedley estate.

On the 1 April 1948, Townend was formally opened to the public for the first time and has continued to introduce visitors to the story of one statesman family ever since. The very first signature in Townend's old visitor book is that of Hugh Dalton. Then chancellor of the exchequer, Dalton had conceived the idea of the National Land Fund – the very thing that allowed Townend to be vested in the National Trust.

Above left Portrait of Clara Browne and her sisters, Lucy and Katherine. Clara is the one standing to the right

Above right Hugh Dalton's signature, the then chancellor of the exchequer, in Townend's old visitor book

Opposite Dresses hanging in one of the servants' bedrooms, discovered when Oswald Hedley undertook a full inventory of the contents of the house

Looking after Townend

Helped by invaluable volunteers, the small team at Townend carries out regular tasks to ensure the building's upkeep.

This includes keeping an eye on light and humidity levels, which can be damaging to the building and collections if not kept at optimal levels. There are also monthly checks for woodworm, mould and other pests – and lots of dusting!

The building project

Every five years, Townend undergoes a 'check-up'. At its 2015 appointment, wet rot was discovered in two beams: slates had degraded and so weren't effectively draining water from the building. Urgent remedial work was required.

But before this could begin, all of the objects in the house had to be carefully packed away into 50 individually labelled crates. Larger objects were rearranged and it took nine people to move the Fire House table.

Then, in April 2016, the building work began. Specialist builders installed temporary supportive frameworks that allowed them to replace the rotten timber and rebuild the stonework around

The collections

As well as keeping an eye on the collections, we also keep detailed records on them. Amongst other information, this includes what the object is and might have been used for, its age and condition. Much of this information can be viewed on the online archive at nationaltrustcollections.org.uk.

them. Removing the render for the first time in 150 years uncovered a wealth of new information about the structure of the house, including: an old fire hood, changes to doors and windows, and bird nesting boxes.

They also uncovered a lead weight placed in the wall where the old front door had been (now displayed in the Fire House). The replacement render was produced by analysing samples to get just the right, and most authentic, mix. The plasterwork inside the house was also repaired and redecorated, and by the end of July 2016, Townend was ready to be re-opened to the public.

Planning for the future

The building project gave us the chance to make other improvements to keep Townend healthy in the future, from trimming back trees and improving air circulation, to better rainwater management and re-rendering the exterior of the house.

Above Townend during the urgent building project in 2016

Left A conservator cleaning one of William Taylor Longmire's sheep paintings

A Taste of Townend

Below A detail from Elizabeth Birkett's 'commonplace book', filled with 57 pages of recipes from the 17th century

In 1699, three years before her marriage to 'Old Ben', Elizabeth Birkett spent a month filling a 57-page book with recipes.

Known as a 'commonplace book', Elizabeth's creation is unremarkable in appearance. Look inside and its content provides a fascinating insight into late 17th-and 18th-century rural life, from foods you might prepare for entertaining to recipes for housekeeping. There are also medicinal cures; with certain afflictions appearing more frequently than others, these give an idea of the ailments most commonly suffered at the time. Even the ingredient lists are intriguing: many seem unusual today, but Elizabeth would have been able to purchase them from local stores and apothecaries.

The medicinal

Some of the recipes are more magical than medicinal. On page three is an instruction to cure 'agues' (fevers): writing abracadabra in a particular arrangement around the neck of the afflicted. The spiced alcoholic concoction *Aqua Mirablis* was said to bring people back from the dead.

Not all the recipes were quite so unusual, or even that dissimilar to ones we use today. Elizabeth's cure for 'herps [sic] … scabs and itches' involves making a balsam from the root of elecampane – a herb recently proven to kill a range of bacteria.

The culinary

Everyday food and recipes were so well known that it's unlikely Elizabeth would have needed to write them down. Instead the culinary recipes in the book – ranging from roasting to baking and brewing – are more sophisticated than day-to-day fare, aimed at entertaining. They feature exotic and extravagant ingredients such as citrus fruits, quinces, venison and anchovies, and spices like nutmeg and cloves, which would have been sold door-to-door by travelling peddlers.

Some recipes are for specific occasions, such as 'wiggs'. These remarkably light, rich, buttery cakes were integral to Westmorland funerals at the time ('Old Ben' purchased over 150 for Elizabeth's funeral in 1728). They were flavoured with caraway seeds to symbolise resurrection and everlasting life. There's also a recipe for bean cakes – these are actually bean-free, instead consisting of a nutty meringue topped with bright comfits and often featured at

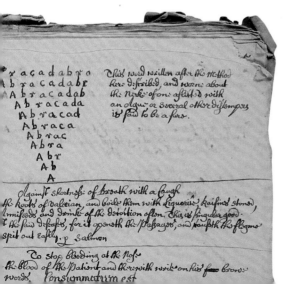

The table in the Downhouse laid out at Christmas with dishes made from Elizabeth's commonplace book

celebrations. The name is perhaps linked to the word 'banns' associated with marriage.

Some of the recipes are still made locally. Consisting of green herbs and leaves, 'green pudding' – also known as Easter Ledges Pudding – is traditionally eaten during Lent and at Easter. The greenery is thought to act like a tonic and bring good health and vitality with the coming of spring.

The household recipes

The household recipes vary hugely in purpose. Everyday remedies, such as using lemon juice as a stain remover, sit alongside instructions for sophisticated crafts such as gilding and japanning. The largest section, however, relates to dyeing. Most colours could be made from plant-based ingredients: tansy for yellow, indigo or heather for green and red from the wildflower madder. The dyes could be made colourfast with a number of different ingredients, but the cheapest and most readily available was 'chamberlye' – urine from chamber pots.

Sharing is caring

Many of Elizabeth's transcribed recipes are taken from other books and Elizabeth's acquaintances. Five came from Dr Salmon's 17th-century home-use medical textbooks, while a cure for nosebleeds is credited at least in part to Sir Thomas Braithwaite of Burneside Hall: it instructs, 'take the blood of the patient and therewith write on his brow the words, *Consummatum est* [it is finished].' (Braithwaite was a known Catholic who had to flee to France after James II was overthrown in 1688.)

Some of the food recipes were also passed on by friends. A Mrs West provided recipes for two types of cakes and one for 'bisketts', and Lady Strickland of Sizergh Castle, Cumbria (now also National Trust) supplied 'sauce for boyld Pikes or any other ffish'. Also Catholics, the Stricklands were friends with Thomas Braithwaite and went with him to France.

Pedigree of the Brownes of Townend

(Owners of Townend are set in **bold** type)

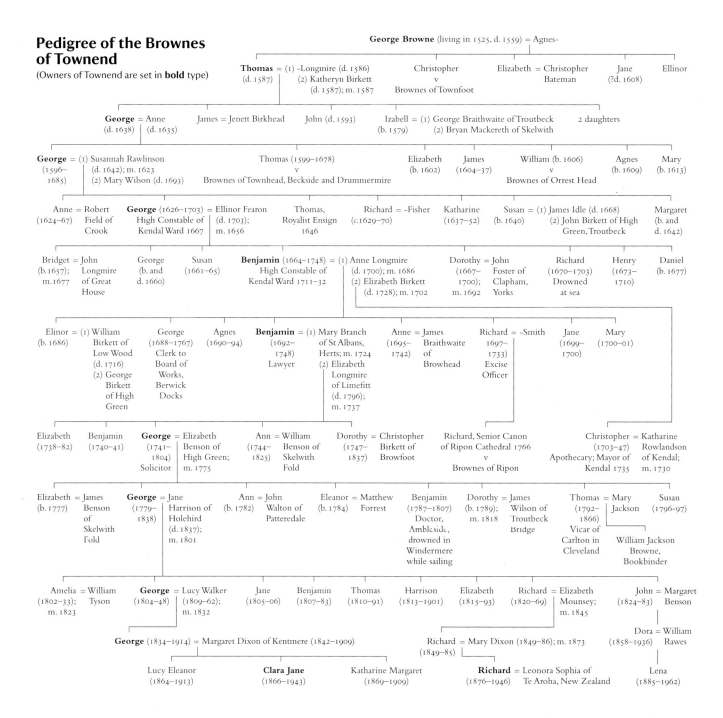